DELIBERATE DECISIONS

A Simple Guide for Real Success

JOYCE BENNETT-HALL

BALBOA.
PRESS

A DIVISION OF HAY HOUSE

Balboa Press books may be ordered through booksellers or by contacting:

Balboa Press
A Division of Hay House
1663 Liberty Drive
Bloomington, IN 47403
www.balboapress.com
1 (877) 407-4847

Because of the dynamic nature of the Internet, any web addresses or links contained in this book may have changed since publication and may no longer be valid. The views expressed in this work are solely those of the author and do not necessarily reflect the views of the publisher, and the publisher hereby disclaims any responsibility for them.

The author of this book does not dispense medical advice or prescribe the use of any technique as a form of treatment for physical, emotional, or medical problems without the advice of a physician, either directly or indirectly. The intent of the author is only to offer information of a general nature to help you in your quest for emotional and spiritual well-being. In the event you use any of the information in this book for yourself, which is your constitutional right, the author and the publisher assume no responsibility for your actions.

Any people depicted in stock imagery provided by Thinkstock are models, and such images are being used for illustrative purposes only. Certain stock imagery © Thinkstock.

Print information available on the last page.

ISBN: 978-1-5043-8397-4 (sc)
ISBN: 978-1-5043-8398-1 (hc)
ISBN: 978-1-5043-8399-8 (e)

Library of Congress Control Number: 2017910847

Balboa Press rev. date: 08/28/2017

Contents

Foreword

It's rare to find a book that provides the step-by-step guidance to take control of our destiny by making empowered, thoughtful choices. *Deliberate Decisions* is that book.

In profoundly simple and highly practical A to Z wisdom, Joyce Bennett-Hall holds nothing back. She shares it all, bringing keen insight to each and every page. Her researched discoveries show us how to turn over-thinking and debilitating procrastination into a deliberate decision. And, it is life changing! Suddenly we find the energy and the presence of mind to say YES to our dreams: no holding back, no painful delays, no gnawing excuses, no self-imposed set backs – only dynamic forward movement.

Simply stated, the methods you'll learn here work. And the specific insights Joyce brings to the page teaches you ways to step past self-sabotaging habits and master high confidence so you can easily put more empowered choices into action – feeling centered, inspired and conscious – laying the foundation to live more fully and gaining the momentum to achieve your best results.

Marsh Engle, Creator of Amazing Living, Author of *The Sacred Agreements and the AMAZING WOMAN multi-book series.*

www.marshengle.com

Introduction

Are there things in your life that you would like to change or add? Do you have goals or dreams you would like to realize in the next week, month, or year? Have you given thanks for all the wonderful things that have happened to you yesterday, last month, or last year? Have you worked through any anger or frustration that might have come about due to the not-so-wonderful things that might have happened during the past year or years? How about your relationships with your family and friends? Have they deepened? Do your relationships with them need more work?

There are books, magazines, lectures, and various other self-improvement modalities that are helpful in answering these questions. Different religions and spiritual philosophies have road maps for how to live life, which are contained in their particular creeds, dogmas, or sacred writings. However, in some cases, these writings are complex and convoluted. *Deliberate Decisions* is a simple and inspiring guide for anyone who wants a complete fulfilling life.

Every year, some of my friends and I visit a boarding school on a Native American Indian reservation in northern Arizona. While visiting a teacher's home, I noticed a piece of paper taped to her bathroom wall. Upon closer inspection, it was an inspirational outline that used the alphabet as a guide for how to live.

As I read the twenty-six sentences, I knew and understood what I was reading. However, it was a reminder to me—sort of a spiritual nudge—to take a look at how I had been living my life. It rang true in my heart that this really is a simple road map for how to live and realize my goals and dreams. After reflecting on my life and these alphabetical sentences, I expanded them to short chapters. I would like to share them with you, and I hope they will inspire you to do some reflecting as well.

TESTIMONIALS

<u>An Awesome Read!</u> This is a must read for everyone. In fact, it is a great book for entry level psychology students.

- Rev. Katherine Bell, Ph.D.D.D.

President, SPICA - Way of Light University of Divinity

<u>Small, but powerful!</u> This is a small, easy to read powerhouse of a book! I love the simplicity and the clarity. On days when I'm not feeling my best, I can pick it up and read a gem on any page and begin to shift my day for the better. The exercises have led me to want to go deeper into self-awareness and self- discovery.

-Kathryn Hack, M.F.T.

Deliberate Decisions is a handbook to self-actualization. This book is a well written, focused, simple, and easy book of promise, a gem offering guidance and inspiration toward becoming our highest and actualized self. Yet, as simple and easy as it is - it is that profound. I am able to use bits and pieces with my counseling clients, as focus for my Sunday messages and most of all - it keeps me ever growing. No matter the level of enlightenment you feel you have obtained - this little book will challenge you to go more deeply toward fulfillment. I recommend *Deliberate Decisions* to individuals personally, counselors for their clients, parents for their teens and group facilitators as a foundation. Joyce Bennett-Hall is a wise and sensitive author and coach. She walks her talk - and this book comes from her own process and journey. It's a great gift of love - for yourself or others.

- Rev. Teri Kierbel

A great guide to living a successful life. The exercises in Joyce's book were very helpful in making the point of each chapter. The exercises improve our perception of reality and make us rethink our experiences from more than one point of view. It helps us take a closer look on another level to pinpoint the target areas of our troubles. When we really get involved, we participate in our own life and make healthier choices because we are able to see the whole picture instead of just a small portion of it. Joyce did an excellent job on the books revision. I am glad that I read it again and I will definitely recommend it to clients and friends!

- Lily-Therese Wiltfong

Deliberate Decisions is About Being Conscious! This simple, clear, powerful little book says so much in such a small space. I love that I can pick it up, open a page and be awakened again to what is important in life. As a Life Success Coach, this will be on my suggested reading list for my clients. I highly recommend it to anyone who wants to know how to grow their life.

- Carolyn Berry, MA, MFT,

Life Success Coach.

Deliberate Decisions is a thought provoking and offers helpful ideas and tips to support and enrich one's life. Each letter addresses a different concept and suggested exercises which inspire and help guide a person forward in life.

- Nicki Coble

What I like best about *Deliberate Decisions* is that I can read just one page and feel better. I keep it on my night table and randomly select a page each evening. No matter which page I choose, there is message of enlightenment.

- Martha Mutz
Retired Teacher

A

Avoid Negative People, Places, And Things.

Negative people rob us of our energy. It takes a lot of energy to live life.

Have you ever felt drained after being with someone who complains about anything and everything? That person is zapping your energy! Avoid those people if possible.

If they're family members and you can't or don't want to avoid them, just listen to them—but don't get caught up in their negative drama. Have shorter visits with them. Give yourself permission to spend less time with them. Think of another A word: *advocate*. Be your own advocate and protect yourself from these energy vampires.

Stay away from negative places that are dangerous or bring up bad memories. Like negative people, negative places can drain our energy and block us from tapping into our creative source.

Avoid negative habits such as excessive drinking or smoking, overeating, or overspending. Get rid of them in any way you can. These habits block your creativity. There are all kinds of resources to help us rid ourselves of negative habits.

Last but not least, avoid negative thinking. Stop criticizing yourself. It's self-defeating. It's okay to tell yourself that you're great because you are great. Your Creator creates only greatness, of which you're a part.

Avoid criticizing and judging other people. Everyone has a story and a path to follow. We're not here to tell other people how to live their lives or to tell them which paths to follow. We're here to create our own stories by following the paths that lead us to becoming the best we can be. Live your life in greatness.

Deliberately decide to avoid these negative sources—and you'll be on your way to success.

Avoid negative people, places, and things.

Deliberate Decisions Exercises

- Think of people in your life who rob you of your energy—people who are complainers, who always see the glass as half empty, or who are just plain negative. Make a list of these people and review it.
- Think of places that bring up negative feelings or feel dangerous to you physically or mentally. Make a list of these places and review it.
- If you have habits that you think are negative and blocking your creativity, write them down and review your list.
- List some of the ways you criticize yourself. At the end of the list, write down some things about yourself that are great.

B

Believe In Yourself.

Sometimes we don't feel very motivated. We feel like we're out of fuel. We start having self-defeating thoughts. Seeing ourselves as failures is easier than visualizing success. We define ourselves by our self-defeating thoughts or images of ourselves. "I'm not good enough." "I'm just not smart enough." "I'm too fat." "I'm too short."

We may blame others for our misgivings or for not reaching our goals. We may blame instead of believing. Blame is giving your power away. Believing in yourself increases your power.

We already know how to achieve our goals. We may not know the details, but we have the overall big picture. Believe in yourself—and the details will fill in. You possess the power to accomplish anything you want. Define yourself by your inner qualities. What you believe about yourself and your life becomes true for you. Believe in yourself. We're part of an amazing tapestry called life. This tapestry is woven with many different designs and colors. Each design is unique and brilliant.

This tapestry would be less rich and less beautiful without you as a part of it. Just knowing that we're part of something so much greater than ourselves gives us the power to create and accomplish anything we set out to do. This power is the fuel that motivates us to reach our goals. Believing we're so much more is the key to the vault that holds our dreams and is the secret to our success.

We all have strengths and weaknesses. We also all have the power to overcome our weaknesses and capitalize on our strengths. Dwelling on negative self-image keeps us from reaching our goals and manifesting our dreams. What we think of ourselves will shape our destinies. Our self-images determine our choices, shape our belief systems, and take over our lives. Self-image becomes a self-fulfilling prophecy.

Believe in yourself and your unique design. Color in this tapestry of life. Let the details fall into place. Never stop believing in yourself. You're the one and only you. You're great—the greatest! You're a perfect piece of art and an important piece of the tapestry.

If you believe that, all things are possible. If you believe in God, a higher power, or something greater than yourself, then ask, "Would my Creator create anything less than perfect?" The answer is no.

We all know about bumper cars. The object of the ride is to bump into as many cars as you can to get them out of your way. Sometimes we drive our vehicles like that. We bump into obstacles that keep us from reaching our goals. We're in the driver's seat of the vehicles we use to get around in life.

If we believe in ourselves, we'll be able to navigate around those obstacles that appear before us on the road to our goals. When we see ourselves as accomplishing anything we wish, the power in the universe supports us, guides us, and propels us toward reaching our goals and dreams.

There is an eternal creative force within us that is waiting to be tapped and channeled into wonderful, joyful creativity. Creative energy can be seen in science, art, literature, and relationships in a positive way. We'll reach our goals and dreams, and we will begin making a difference in the world.

Deliberately decide to believe in yourself. You're truly wonderful. Be full of wonder—and you'll fulfill your dreams!

Believe in yourself.

Deliberate Decisions Exercises

- Since a belief is nothing more than a feeling of absolute certainty about what something means, your beliefs can help you reach your goals. They can also hinder you. They can be unconscious or conscious, and they often stem from things you've heard, seen, or felt a lot of emotion about. You may have repeated them to yourself until you felt certain they were true.
- Write down all the old beliefs that have kept you from following through on your goals in the past.
- Make a list of new beliefs that will empower you from this day forward.

C

Consider Your Goals And Dreams From All Angles.

Goals or dreams may change from time to time. Sometimes they change while we're on the path to realizing them, or they may change at the moment we realize them. However, each time we set a new goal, we should consider things from every angle. We must consider things from the heart as well as intellectually.

We may ask, "Does this goal or dream express all aspects of who I am? Does it embody all that I am spiritually, mentally, emotionally, and physically?" If the goal or dream doesn't, you may fail in achieving your goal or manifesting your dream. You could end up following a dream or reaching for a goal that doesn't support your highest good.

Our lives consist of four aspects: spiritual, mental, emotional, and physical. The spiritual level provides a foundation for the development of other levels. Make sure your goals are in alignment with your universal life source—your oneness with life—and they'll support your highest good.

Your mind holds all of your beliefs and values. Ask yourself, "Am I conscious of my thought patterns? Do I have a clear understanding of my belief system? Do my beliefs, values, and philosophies support my highest good?" If you become aware of any beliefs, values, or philosophies that fall short, you may want to do some work on this level before considering the next one.

Since the ability to relate to others and the world on a feeling level comes from an emotional level, we want to be aware of what and how we feel at any given time. Am I fulfilled in my relationship with myself and others? If you're not aware or fulfilled, you may need to do some emotional healing work before continuing on your journey to realize your goal or dream.

The final aspect to consider is our physical bodies. This includes the ability to survive and thrive in this world. "Have I developed the skills to live comfortably and effectively in the world?" "Am I in tune with my body?" "Do I listen to what my body is telling me?" Our bodies know what they need. If we listen, they communicate clearly and specifically. "Am I understanding and interpreting my body's signals correctly?"

If we're aligned spiritually, have a clear understanding of our values and beliefs, have a good relationship with ourselves and others, and understand our physical needs, we're ready for the journey to success!

Consider your goals and dreams from all angles.

Deliberate Decisions Exercises

- List some of the goals you want to reach.
- Review the list. Do they support you spiritually? Do they support your highest good? Are they in alignment with your chosen spiritual path?
- Review your goals list again. Do they support you mentally? Do they support your beliefs and values?
- Review your goals list one more time. Do they support you emotionally? Do your goals assist you or block you from being aware of what you feel at any given time? Do they support you or keep you from being fulfilled in your relationships with yourself and others?
- Review your goals list a final time. Do your goals support you physically? Since your ability to survive and thrive in the world depends on the skills you acquire, do your goals assist and support you with developing these skills? Are your goals in alignment with your physical health or financial security?
- Revisit any goals that don't support all four of these areas: spiritual, mental, emotional, and physical.

D

Don't Give Up. Dare To Succeed.

We all want to reach our goals and manifest our dreams. However, some people reach them, and some don't. Why is that? Why aren't we all what we want to be? Well, we all have a list of excuses and use them as reasons for why we are not successful or living our dream. The A section of this book talks about how negative self-talk is self-defeating. Negative self-talk translates into why we are not living up to our full potential. Go through your list of self-defeating excuses for why you fall short of your goals.

"I don't have the education," "I'm bald," or "I am too old" may sound familiar. These are excuses—not reasons. We fear setting goals. What if we don't make it? What if we fail? We will be embarrassed! Fear is what stops us all!

We can have anything we want if we tell ourselves what we want and direct our conscious minds to reach for it. Once we do that, the subconscious mind will take over and figure out the details.

There was a man who was born in 1809 in a log cabin in Kentucky. His parents were born in Virginia of undistinguished families. When he was seven years old, his family moved to Indiana. His younger brother and mother died shortly thereafter. Several years later, his older sister died in childbirth. He moved to Illinois in 1830 and worked several jobs, including surveyor, postmaster, and shopkeeper. He made an unsuccessful run for the Illinois legislature in 1832.

The store went out of business, and he purchased another store with a partner. This venture ultimately failed, leaving him badly in debt. Two years later, his former partner died, increasing his debt. That very same year, the lady he loved died from fever.

He married in 1842, and the union produced four children. Only one reached adulthood. The man had many political setbacks before he was ultimately elected as the sixteenth US president. His name was Abraham Lincoln.

After Lincoln's election, many Southern states, fearing Republican abolition of slavery, seceded from the Union. Lincoln faced the greatest internal crisis of any US president. After the fall of Fort Sumter, Lincoln raised an army and fought to save the Union from falling apart.

Initially, Lincoln anticipated a short conflict. He called for 75,000 volunteers to serve for three months. Despite enormous pressures, loss of life, battlefield setbacks, poor generals, and assassination threats, Lincoln stuck with this pro-Union policy for four long years of civil war. On January 1, 1863, the Emancipation Proclamation declared freedom for all slaves in the Confederacy. Lincoln never gave up!

Abraham Lincoln is remembered for his vital role in preserving the Union during the Civil War and ending slavery in the United States. He is also remembered for his character. He was a man of humble origins whose determination and perseverance led him to the nation's highest office.

Don't give up—no matter what. Dare to succeed!

Don't give up. Dare to succeed.

Deliberate Decisions Exercises

- What have you given up on in the past? Why do you think you gave up?
- What fears are in the way of you reaching your goal(s)?
- Finally, write down some things that you have accomplished, achieved, or done successfully in your life. Congratulate yourself for what you have achieved and use your successes to inspire you toward your goals.

E

Enthusiasm Matters.

Enthusiasm means "one with the energy of God." It derives from root words relating to being inspired and possessed by the Divine. There is something awesome about people practicing this spiritual quality. They are vibrantly alive.

In *Spiritual Literacy*, Mary Ann Brussat includes a story written by Margret M. Stevens about three brick masons who are busy at work. When the first is asked what he is building, he answers without looking up, "I'm laying bricks." The second replies, "I'm building a wall." But the third responds with great enthusiasm, "I am building a cathedral." Enthusiasm lights up your life and the lives of those around you.

In an essay, newspaper columnist Linda Weltner wrote, "Modern life can grow dull and predictable … still there's one magic talisman left that has the power to bring freshness, novelty, and surprise into your life. Someone else's enthusiasm."

Look at the meaning of the word through the words of scientist Louis Pasteur: "The Greeks have given us one of the most beautiful words of our language, the word enthusiasm— a God within. The grandeur of the acts of men is measured by the inspiration from which they spring. Happy is he who bears a God within."

Each and every one of us is exactly where we are in life, according to the consciousness we hold. If you don't like where you are in your life—or your goals seem unattainable—you must find your consciousness. Consciousness is the root of enthusiasm. Become enthusiastic about life, and you will enjoy all of life's riches. Enthusiasm propels us forward on our path toward our goals.

There are other E words we can incorporate into our way of living. *Excitement* is one. Be excited about life itself. Be excited about your goals. Excitement leads to enthusiasm. Taking the journey enthusiastically shortens the road to your goals.

Another E word is *entitlement*.

Do you believe you are entitled to your dreams, your goals, or abundant living? Do you believe the Divine Presence, or God, as you understand God to be, is all around you as a fish lives in water? If so, can the fish of the sea ever lack for water? Can we be in the sea of Divine Presence or the energy of God and ever lack a sufficient amount of creativity, ideas, money, or opportunities in times of need? The answer is no. You must believe you are entitled to your goals and dreams, get excited about them, and take your journey with enthusiasm. If you do, your success is guaranteed!

Enthusiasm matters.

Deliberate Decisions Exercises

- How enthusiastic are you about your life? List some things about your life that you are enthusiastic about.
- List some things that you are not enthusiastic about.
- How can you change the things about your life that you are not enthusiastic about? Write them down.
- There is another E word you might want to consider. Take a look at your spiritual economics. List your views on affluence. Prosperity in the broadest sense can mean "spiritual well-being" or "healthy spiritual economics." Upon reviewing your list, do you have the consciousness to attract the things you want in your life? If not, what changes could you make in your thinking to increase your spiritual well-being?

F

Family And Friends Are Treasures. Seek Out Their Riches.

Families come in all shapes and forms. Some consist of a mother and father, some have just one parent, and some have a grandparent or guardian. No matter how your family looks, seek out the riches of their treasures. They will assist you on your journey toward reaching your goals.

Even though family encouragement and inspiration are obvious riches, there are hidden treasures in the challenges we may face with our families. These challenges help you grow spiritually and emotionally. The more you grow and become aware of your own power, the easier reaching your goals and dreams become.

You also have another family—the human family. Each person in this family has a gift for you. Take the time to find it.

I was on a flight to Phoenix, Arizona. There was a young man with Down's syndrome in the middle seat, and his caretaker was in the window seat. It was obvious that people were avoiding the aisle seat next to him. I decided to sit and appreciate being near the front of the plane. Well, this young man offered me the most delightful gift of being a new friend. He told me his name, and it was quite obvious he was nervous about the takeoff. We chatted, and by the time we started to taxi, we had become fast friends.

I asked if he would like to hold hands during takeoff. He said yes, and we did. We held hands for quite a while after takeoff and continued to talk with the help of his caretaker since he had trouble articulating his thoughts. His mom and sister had died, and he was going to live with his cousin. He told me about his dog and how he liked having pretzels in the evening. He liked to take a shower, get into his pajamas, and watch television before bed. Even though he was difficult to understand verbally, I understood what his heart was saying. I felt connected to it.

Sadness came over me when we started to land. I knew my new friend and I would part soon. In the terminal, we waved good-bye and went our separate ways. He will live in my heart always.

All people we meet are part of our human family. They bring us gifts. Accept them. They will enrich your life and assist you on your journey toward reaching your goals. Determining what that gift means is up to you. It may not take the form you expect. Make a deliberate decision to seek out the treasures in all people.

Family and friends are treasures. Seek out their riches.

Deliberate Decisions Exercises

- Make a list of your immediate family. What riches do they offer you? Write them down next to each name.
- Make a list of your extended family. What riches do they offer you? Write them down next to each name.
- Make a list of some of your close friends. What riches do they offer you? Write them down next to each name.
- Make a list of other friends and acquaintances in your life. What riches do they offer you?

G

Give More Than You Planned.

The ABCs. How simple life is really. Life isn't out to *get* any of us. Life doesn't favor any of us. Life just happens. Life doesn't pick and choose whose dreams or goals will be realized. Life is how we view it. It is a perceptual experience. Perceive it as perfect, and it is perfect. How we experience life—how we perceive life—is in direct relation to what we give in life. Giving and receiving are two sides of the same coin.

To complete a gift, there must be a giver who truly wants to give and a receiver who wants to receive. The giver creates a vacuum after giving and is now ready to receive. The recipient is in a position to give. The receiver need not give something back to the same person. Both giver and receiver keep the flow of giving and receiving going and allow everything to move freely in and out of their lives. Holding on to anything blocks the flow like the ebb and flow of the tides in the ocean. It is a cycle.

Visualize a circle of people with each person giving to and receiving from another person in the circle. If one person holds on too long, the flow stops—and everyone in the circle feels the block in energy. When everything moves freely around the room, everyone receives the benefits as well as the energy that circulates.

Earlier, we talked about family. We are all part of this human family. We are in relationships of different types in this human family. If we don't get what we want in our relationships, we need to look at what we give. Giving is an important part of receiving. The way we give to others is the way the universe will give to us. Giving money, things, or love is truly a gift to yourself. It creates a circulation of energy in your life. When more energy circulates, you are wealthier in all aspects of life.

If more money is a goal, give money. If a new job is a goal, think about what you give to your current job.

Giving affirms abundance and helps us feel prosperous. If we wrap our hands around money, our hands are not open to receive more.

Gratitude is the partner of giving. When we feel grateful, we are in a state of happiness. We are kinder, more generous, and friendlier. This behavior makes your life better automatically and helps you to live your life more fully.

Time seems to collapse as we attain our goals since people who reflect your thoughts, feelings, and experiences seem to be drawn to you. Gratitude reflects back to us in wonderful ways. In the Eastern philosophy, it is known as Karma, the currency of life. With Karma, we purchase and create our life experiences: good, bad, pleasant, or unpleasant.

Deliberately decide to give more than you planned—whether it is love, money, time, kindness, or friendship. Give more than you planned to give. Give without expectations. Give without condition—and then give more—and then give even more. Remember to be grateful for what you have.

Give more than you planned.

Deliberate Decisions Exercises

- What percentage of your financial income you are tithing?
- Do you tithe some of your time by volunteering? If not, make a list of places you could do some volunteer work.
- Create a daily gratefulness journal. Write down five things you are grateful for each day.

H

Hang On To Your Goals And Dreams.

Hang on to your goals and dreams—no matter what. Hang in there—like a cat hanging from a tree branch. When my goals and dreams seem so far away, I remember that poor cat every time. When I feel discouraged, I hang in there—even when it feels like I'm hanging by my fingernails.

Obstacles get in the way on the road to our dreams. We may feel like we can't move them. If we can't move them, we can go around them. We waste precious time and energy trying to move the unmovable.

I met a man who dreamed of becoming a marathon runner. He faced major challenges when he got older, but he clung to his dream. He practiced under some grueling circumstances. Even though the pain was almost unbearable, he continued to train.

It took him several years to become conditioned enough to participate in a marathon. He took his place at the starting line. Although he came in last, he finished the race. As he crossed the finish line, the spectators and other participants cheered him on. He had no feet. Can you imagine the obstacles he had to overcome to reach his dream? He overcame them because he hung on to his dream. Deliberately decide to hang on to yours!

Hang on to your goals and dreams.

Deliberate Decisions Exercises

- Are you avoiding people who don't support your goals and dreams?
- Do you believe in yourself?
- Are you daring to succeed?
- Are you excited about your goals?
- If the answer to any of these questions is no, I suggest rereading the chapter that applies. Keep applying the principles addressed in these chapters to encourage you to hang on to your goals and dreams.

I

Ignore The Opinions Of Others.

Avoid sharing your goals with people who say things like, "Why would you want to do that?"

Have you ever said, "Boy, I have a great idea," shared it, and had someone give a negative opinion about it? Do you remember how you felt? Did you feel empowered? Did you feel as enthused about your idea after hearing that negative opinion? Of course not. We give our power away if we listen to negativity. Life will not be as rich. Goals and dreams may never come to fruition. Success will elude us.

Our obsessive need for acceptance and approval from other people hinders us from realizing our goals. This need permeates all areas of our lives. It affects our relationships and our careers. It affects how we spend our money, the way we dress, and the way we respond to loved ones and strangers. It can affect the kind of food we eat and what time we wake up. The need to please other people causes us to have unsatisfying lifestyles and remain in unsupportive relationships. Carried to the extreme, this need to please others can cause illness, poverty, and death.

If we run our lives based on what other people think of us, we destroy our own self-creativity. We destroy our essence. If we live our lives to please others, we chip away at ourselves. If we focus our energies on pleasing other people and allow the opinions of others to matter, our lives will be less than magnificent. If we live to please, our lives will be full of confusion and dissatisfaction.

Ignoring the opinions of others does not mean not listening to anything. Refusing to listen closes the door on opportunities to learn. Use what people think of you or your ideas as a guide for your life. Reflecting on what someone else says about us gives a clearer view of ourselves and allows for personal growth. Avoid using the input from others to feel guilty, wrong, or insecure. When we change to please others, the vicious circle begins.

We can use the views of others to reinforce negative mental patterns or get rid of what we don't want. Choosing the latter gives us opportunities for growth in every area of our lives. Growing and improving are the foundations for our success. Avoid listening to the voice of fear. We hear it in other people's negative opinions. Listen to your own inner voice of courage. That voice will keep you moving on the path to success.

Ignore the opinions of others.

Deliberate Decisions Exercises

- What don't you do because you're afraid of what other people might think?
- What do you continue doing because you're afraid of what other people might think?
- Review your lists and reflect on what you wrote. Go out and do the things you have been afraid to do, stop doing what you don't want to do, and ignore the opinions of others!

J

Just Take Action!

Procrastination is your worst enemy when it comes to living life fully, reaching your goals, and realizing your dreams. Reaching them requires action. We can dream, visualize, and write affirmations about meeting our goals.

Unless we take action, we will not realize them.

If you want to sing, get a voice coach and take lessons. If you want to be an attorney, go to school and study the law. Professional race car drivers, golfers, and other athletes take the steps necessary to become what they are. They take action!

We may get stuck and not know what to do next. It actually doesn't matter what we do—just do something! We will get the energy moving around us. The stimulation of energy will guide us.

Take a risk! Take a chance! Goals are met, and dreams are realized by risk-takers—not by people who play it safe. You can't lose if you take action! Deliberately decide to do so!

Just take action!

Deliberate Decisions Exercises

- If you only had three months to live—and you knew for certain you would not live a day beyond that time—what would you do during those three months?
- Why aren't you doing those things now?
- Make a list of things that you have been procrastinating about.
- Pick one thing on your list and take action toward accomplishing it.

K

Keep On Going.

Sometimes we get tired. Sometimes life overwhelms us. We can't seem to get out of the pain caused by loss. Perhaps we lost a child in the Middle East conflict or a daughter to illness or a job or a marriage we thought would last forever.

How can we continue on the journey toward our goals when we are so overwhelmed? How can we continue when we are in so much pain?

When a situation looks hopeless, keep hoping. Don't quit. Keep going. When everything looks impossible, refuse to accept defeat.

Don't quit. Keep going. People who succeed in the face of seemingly impossible conditions are people who don't know how to quit. What can we do when unexpected changes wreak havoc on our dreams? Avoid dwelling on loss. If you do, you will be discouraged and defeated. Instead of thinking about loss, concentrate on what you have left.

I want to share a story about refusing to quit. Walter Greving, a handsome northwest Iowan, suffered a severe bout of polio. When the disease left him, he took stock of the permanent damage. His chest muscles were paralyzed. He would spend the rest of his life on an artificial respirator. Walter's arms, legs, hands, and shoulders were all permanently paralyzed. However, he could still see, think, hear, and talk. He still had the use of a single finger. Instead of dwelling on what he lost, he thought, *What can I do with what I have left? What can I do with one finger?*

He thought, *I could push a button that opens up an almost unlimited assortment of possibilities.*

A button started a tape recorder and enabled him to dictate encouraging letters that he sent around the world. A tape recorder, a radio, a TV, and a book-page flipper could all be enjoyed by using just one finger.

He said, "I was never happier before polio than I am today. I never really started to live until I got into the iron lung. I learned to think differently. I didn't quit. I didn't give up. I kept going."

Whenever you feel like giving up or packing it in, think of Walter Greving—and keep going!

Keep on going.

Deliberate Decisions Exercises

- If you haven't written down your goals, do so now. Write them on a card, carry it with you, and look at it whenever you can.

- If one of your goals is a material item, place a picture of it somewhere you can see it often. Write down motivational sayings on several cards, place them in your home and work area, and look at them often.

- For each goal you want to achieve, write a paragraph about why you want to achieve it. Include the reasons why you must and will achieve them.

- What are some of the things you may need to do that you don't want to do in order to achieve these goals? Write them down.

- Review your list of goals. Ask yourself if you are committed to achieving your goals. Do you have the passion to do anything it takes to achieve them? If you do, identify one small thing you can do immediately toward achieving one of your goals.

- Review your list of the things you may need to do that you don't want to do in order to achieve your goals. Decide which thing you will do this week toward achieving one of your goals.

- To make sure you follow through, tell someone what and when you are going to do it. Now you've got your momentum back.

L

Love Yourself.

This may be a strange concept for some. It may even seem self-indulgent. Before we reach any of our goals, we must feel worthy enough to receive them.

If we think, "I'm too fat," "I'll never amount to anything," "I'm too old," or "I'm not good enough," we undermine our self-image. We fail to reach our goals. If we feel too fat, we can start a weight-loss program. Worrying about our weight takes focus off our goals. If debt stops you from doing what you want, start a financial plan and focus on prosperity. If we feel too old or too young or that we don't deserve what we want, then reaching our goal is impossible until we change our focus from the negative to the positive.

Yes, there are some things we cannot change. However, we can change our perception of ourselves. See the power and creativity instead of limitations. Fake it until you make it. Start looking in the mirror in the morning and say, "I love you and accept you just the way you are. You are worthy of receiving your goals and dreams." Fake it until you believe it. Start embodying the positive feelings of loving yourself.

Love yourself enough to set good boundaries. Say "no" to people who want to use you or your time. Limit your time with people who do not support your goals. Avoid abusive people. What are other boundaries? How do you use your time? Are you focused on your goals? Do you waste time doing things that hinder your progress?

Loving ourselves allows our goals and dreams to flourish in direct proportion to the positive perceptions we have of ourselves. We are wonderful, powerful, and creative. We are worthy of having goals and dreams fulfilled. We are born for success!

Love yourself.

Deliberate Decisions Exercises

- Write down at least eight things you can do to show how much you love yourself. Write yourself a love letter.
- For the next fourteen days, take several minutes each morning to look in the mirror and say, "I love you, (your name), and accept you just as your are."
- Write down some of the specific reasons why you love yourself.

M

Meditate And Make It Happen.

Using the ABCs is a fun way to learn and acquire the necessary tools for reaching our goals. Each letter holds a vital insight into life. M is one more letter that we can use to enrich our life. We can use M for *meditating* or *making it happen*, or both. Each has its own meaning, but they work in concert with each other.

Meditating in the morning sets the tone for the day and helps us live in the moment. When we live life in the moment, we make life work. When we live in the now, we surrender and allow inspiration to be our motivation in achieving our goals.

When you make things happen from your own will—your ego place—you may find the goals from that place are not fulfilling. When we are open and allow ourselves to receive inspiration, life will offer us many riches.

Meditation helps us become aware of our higher selves. We start seeing our highest selves as a dimension of being that transcends the limitation of the physical world. Our highest selves have the capacity to attract all we need or desire.

Be one with your environment. See yourself as part of everyone and everything. Harness the power that makes things happen. Trust in the wisdom that created us. Trust in the wisdom that lives in our hearts and not our heads. Meditate on that wisdom and make it happen.

Meditate and make it happen.

Deliberate Decisions Exercises

- Start meditating for ten minutes each day for the next two weeks. If you haven't meditated before, light a candle and watch the flame flicker for those ten minutes.
- Write down your experience after each meditation.
- For the next two weeks, meditate for fifteen minutes each day. Try it without the candle.
- Continue to write down your experiences after each meditation.
- Close your eyes, take in a deep breath, hold it, and then slowly release it.
- Take another deep breath, hold it, and then slowly release it.
- Do this several more times. With each breath, visualize yourself breathing in all the positive energy in the universe. When you slowly release it, visualize yourself breathing out any negative thoughts or feelings you might be holding.
- Start relaxing your body by sending positive energy to your feet, your calves, and then your knees. Feel them letting go and relaxing. Send that positive energy to your thighs, your abdomen, and then your arms and hands. Feel them letting go of any physical tightness and relaxing. Send positive energy to your heart. Feel your heart opening and being ready to receive all the wonderful things the universe has to offer you. Send positive energy to your neck, your shoulders, and then your head. Feel the muscles letting go in your neck,

your shoulders, and your head. Let the positive energy flow all through your body.

- Visualize a beautiful light. Watch the light as it grows until it fills the entire inner vision of your mind. See the special place of peace within the beautiful light. It could be a temple, a mountain, a beach, a park, or any other safe place to share and receive. Get comfortable in this safe place. Invite God—as you understand God, Spirit, or whoever you feel comfortable talking to—and share any concerns or problems. After you ask for advice, listen. Continue the dialog as long as it is comfortable for you.

- When you are done, say, "Thank you for coming—and for the words you have spoken to me. Good-bye." You can start leaving your safe place. You will see that beautiful golden light again and watch it start to disappear. When you are ready go back to the room, open your eyes and write down your experience.

N

Never Lie, Cheat, Or Steal.
Always Strike A Fair Deal.

This letter represents one of the most powerful insights into how to create success. Lying, cheating, and stealing come from fear—not power. These qualities shouldn't represent who you are.

We have all come from that place at one time or another. If we are honest with ourselves, we acknowledge the difficulty in keeping a lie going. We put much energy into keeping our lies real. Lying wastes energy.

Cheating does not stem from our highest consciousness. Cheating hurts the cheated—and it hurts the cheater. Cheating diminishes integrity. Cheating produces empty victories.

Stealing takes many forms. It can be stealing time from our jobs or giving away food to your friends at a restaurant. Many people don't see either one as stealing. Everyone agrees about the obvious stealing of property or money. Stealing limits our ability to create what we want in our lives.

Lying, cheating, and stealing are roadblocks on our journeys. They keep us from reaching our destinations.

Always play fair in business and in your personal life. Integrity and honesty are our calling cards when dealing with others. When we act from our highest consciousness, we are in the most powerful creative place we can be—and our victories are glorious.

Never lie, cheat, or steal. Always strike a fair deal.

Deliberate Decisions Exercises

- Reflect on your behavior in your past jobs. Did you ever do personal business on an employer's time or make excessive personal phone calls? What other behaviors might have been interpreted as stealing? Write them down.

- Have you ever taken something that wasn't yours from a person or a business? Reflect on the times that this behavior occurred. What was going on in your life at that time? Write down the behavior and what was going on in your life at that time.

- Have you had something taken from you? What? How did you feel? Write down what was taken and how that action made you feel.

- Since your level of integrity is your calling card, write down how you would like others to view you. What does your calling card say?

O

Open Your Eyes To See Things As They Really Are.

Life is all about perception. How we perceive things is how we conceive things. If we are so busy focusing on the trivial, we might not see the forest for the trees. If we go through life looking but not really seeing, we might miss golden opportunities. We might miss the chance to reach our goals. We might miss opportunities for success.

There is so much to see if we really learn to look. Think about the last person you saw on the street who you presumed to be homeless. Were the person's clothes tattered? Did the person need a bath or a shave? That is just the surface. What are the eyes of your heart seeing? Open them up and see this person as someone with a story to tell and lessons to teach. This person needs love—just like you do. Look with your heart and see what is really there.

When I was a young girl, my father served in the military. We moved several times due to his transfers. At one place, I spent many afternoons on the porch with an elderly man who shared stories from his youth. He was blind and told me he really did not see until he lost his sight. He was not born blind. It was amazing to hear how he saw life through the eyes of his heart. He had taken his sight for granted. His words have guided me through my life.

When I look at a tree, I take time to see the bark. I look carefully at all the life that moves in and around that bark. When I look at the leaves, I look closely at the veins. I see how they make intricate designs within the leaves. I see how they attach to the branches. I see how the branches weave in and around the tree like beautiful pieces of art.

Take time to look closely at someone. Notice the person's eyes, smile, and expression. These are the windows into who the person really is and what he or she is feeling. The windows let you into someone's heart.

As a young girl, that blind elderly man really touched my heart. Since then, I try to see with my heart. I pass his words to you. Open your eyes to see things as they really are. Appreciate everyone and everything in nature as a piece of art. Your success will be your creative masterpiece.

Open your eyes to see things as they really are.

Deliberate Decisions Exercises

- Take a walk through a forest or a park or hike on a nature trail. Take note of what you see. Are there trees? Flowers? Birds? Ground squirrels? What do you see? Pay attention to all the details of each thing you see. Write them down. And leave your cell phone at home!

- When meeting someone for the first time, pretend you have to introduce this person to someone without describing his or her obvious physical features. How would you go about doing that? Where would you start? Maybe look into the person's eyes and listen to what your heart is telling you.

- Make a list of all the things you focus on that really don't matter. Review this list and see how they are blocking your real vision.

- Have you missed any opportunities in your life because you were focusing on something that really didn't matter? If so, write down those missed opportunities. Review the list and decide to focus on your goals and dreams.

P

Practice Makes Perfect.

Whatever your personal goal or dream—or whatever riches in life you want to embrace—practice, practice, and practice more. It takes practice to accomplish your goals.

Practice takes work. I took piano lessons when I was young, and I performed in recitals. I hated to practice, but I knew I wouldn't know how to play the song if I didn't practice. Since I didn't want to be embarrassed, I practiced, practiced, and practiced more.

Practice makes perfect denotes *work*. Without practice, living a full life just doesn't happen.

The famous fliers known as the Thunderbirds perform at air shows with maneuvers that form art in the sky. They practice flying every day. Many maneuvers are very hard on their bodies, but their goal is to perform as a squadron and be the very best. That is their goal and their dream. They practice, practice, and practice more.

Another kind of practice is practicing presence or being in the now. The secret of harmonious living or manifesting a rich, full life is living in the now. It is living in this moment. We must develop a spiritual consciousness of the now. We must develop a consciousness free from fear, anxiety, anger, jealousy, gossip, and judgment. When we judge, gossip, or come from negative feelings, we don't live in the present. We are living in the past or wondering about the future. It takes practice to develop spiritual consciousness and live in the moment.

Living in our highest consciousness takes practice. Reaching goals or living life more fully may seem to demand greater strength, knowledge, and abilities. There may be greater financial demands than we can meet. Keep focused on what you want. Avoid the "I can't" trap. We can do anything we put our minds to.

Practice living in the moment. Develop the consciousness to support your dreams. Practice holding the highest-quality thoughts. We must rid ourselves of anger, judgment, and fear. Remember your dreams! Embrace a higher level of consciousness to start living in the now.

According to Eckhart Tolle, when we come from anger, can't forgive someone, or we can't accept others as they are, we are not living in the present. If you are upset or tempted to judge another person, stop and ask, "Am I coming from my highest place right now?" If your answer is no, start developing a higher consciousness. Experience the harmony that comes from living in the present—and practice, practice, and practice more.

Practice makes perfect.

Deliberate Decisions Exercises

- Living in the present moment is sometimes very difficult. Practice living in the moment with these suggested exercises. When listening to music, pay attention to the words, rhythms, and sentiments. When taking a shower, be very mindful of the water coming out of the showerhead. Feel every drop of water that hits your body. Inhale and exhale slowly while feeling the water coming down on you. When finished, give thanks for the opportunity to experience the water in such a mindful way.

- When taking care of basic chores around your house—doing the dishes, cleaning, or washing clothes—consider each chore the most important thing in life. Treat each chore as a sacred action. When you are finished, give thanks for the opportunity to experience these tasks. Get a piece of paper and a pencil, set a timer for ten minutes, sit quietly, and focus only on positive thoughts. Every time a negative thought comes into your mind, make a little mark on your paper. If you judge yourself for thinking that negative thought, make another mark on the paper.

- At the end of the ten minutes, count the marks on your paper. How many marks do you have? Multiply that number by six—and that is how many negative thoughts you have in an hour. You can continue to multiply the hours by the day, week, month, and year if you want. The point of this exercise is to make you aware of your negative thinking.

- Pay attention to any negative thoughts that come into your mind this week. At that moment, ask it to leave or replace it with a positive one. Continue this exercise each day until it becomes a habit. Eliminate negative thinking and replace it with positive thoughts.

- If your goal requires learning a new skill, practice working on that new skill every day for the next thirty days.

Q

Quitters Never Win—And Winners Never Quit.

Every time we feel like giving up on our goals, forgetting our dreams, and quitting, think of all the people who influence our lives in wonderful and positive ways because they didn't quit. They may have experienced many trials and tribulations before reaching their goals.

Orville and Wilbur Wright never gave up. They endured many years of research, disappointments, and disasters before their first model flying machine flew more than five minutes. That was in

1904, and it was the beginning of aviation. No one would have blamed them if they had given up and quit. They didn't, and because they didn't, we have air travel today. They were winners.

Summers in the 1950s were full of fear and anxiety for many parents when children by the thousands became infected with crippling polio. Through many painstaking years of research, Dr. Jonas Salk discovered a vaccine. He didn't quit searching. He was a winner—and so were the children saved by his vaccine.

Think about Alexander Graham Bell, the father of telecommunications, or Dr. Martin Luther King Jr. and the civil rights movement. Go back to striving toward your goal. If you don't quit, it is a win-win situation for everyone. If your dreams come true, you may contribute to society in some wonderful way too.

Think about someone you respect and admire for his or her tenacity. Think about someone who didn't quit. Think about people who kept going until they reached their goals and saw their dreams come true. Use them as mentors. Remember "that quitters don't win—and winners don't quit."

Quitters never win—and winners never quit.

Deliberate Decisions Exercises

- Research famous people and review their stories until you find someone who had many seemingly impossible obstacles to overcome. Choose someone who never quit going toward his or her goal. Write at least one paragraph about the qualities that kept this person going.
- Review your writing and use it as a motivator when you feel like quitting.
- List the qualities you have that will keep you from quitting.
- Use your list as a motivator toward becoming a winner.

R

Read, Study, And Learn What Is Important In Your Life.

Embrace and appreciate acquired knowledge. Take classes, go to seminars, and join study groups. Study and learn from anyone that helps you on your journey toward fulfilling your dreams.

Give yourself permission to read books in any way you want. Peruse, skip around, or read the chapters you want. Reading is more enjoyable that way, and learning can be more fun.

When we are in school or learning new jobs, we need to read and learn to graduate or complete our jobs. When we read or learn about our passion and what makes our hearts sing, reading and learning take on whole new meanings.

If one of your goals is to learn more about religion, you may want to read inspirational writings from other cultures, religions, and philosophies. Sutras are words set in prose that speak to Buddhists. The Upanishads in Hinduism are prose texts and dialogues. The *Tao Te Ching*, the written principle of Taoism meaning the Way and the Virtue, is written like a prayer book and speaks about the Tao, the way, the force, an energy, a power. In Christianity, the New Testament shares the gospels and the teachings of Jesus. All these writings can teach us about religious belief systems.

If your goal is to fly a plane, you can read about the mechanics of a plane in addition to taking flying lessons. If your goal is opening a restaurant, you can read about management as well as cuisine. You can learn about mythology. Reading books by experts teaches us about mythological stories, symbols, and life.

No matter what your goals are, read, study, and learn.

Read, study, and learn what is important in your life.

Deliberate Decisions Exercises

- Write down how you spend your time. Next to each item, write down how much time you spend doing it.
- Review your list. Are you spending too much time on things that will not assist you in achieving your goals?
- What are you currently reading? Are you reading books, articles, or journals that will help you acquire the knowledge you need to achieve your goals?
- What have you learned in the last month? Will this knowledge help you achieve your goals? Are you taking any classes or going to seminars that will help you achieve your goals?
- For the next week, spend less time on the things that will not help you achieve your goals and more time reading or studying materials that will assist you.
- Do you know anyone who has already accomplished or achieved any of your goals and dreams? If possible, talk to them and learn from them.

S

Stop Procrastinating.

We procrastinate for many reasons. We procrastinate because we fear failure. We procrastinate because we feel unworthy of fulfillment. It really doesn't matter why we procrastinate—we need to stop. Our success depends on it.

Take action! Any action is better than inaction. What are you putting off that needs doing to get what you want? Is it something you don't like to do, something you think takes too long, or something you feel embarrassed about? It really doesn't matter why. Action is the only cure.

Procrastination keeps us from new jobs, new relationships, and making enough money to buy a new house or new car. Stop right now! Think of three tasks to help you get going. Even small tasks help—including writing a long overdue letter or folding laundry.

Write down three small tasks down after reading this chapter. Pick one to do before going on to the next letter. If we procrastinate about writing down and choosing one small task right now, think about what procrastination costs in the big picture. We cannot walk the path toward our goals with our feet in buckets of cement. Those buckets represent procrastination. Chip away at the cement, free your feet, and get moving!

Stop procrastinating.

Deliberate Decisions Exercises

- What are three simple things you could do that you have been putting off? Write them down.
- Pick one thing and do it today.
- Reward yourself.
- List two new actions you could take to help you achieve your goals.
- Pick one of these actions and accomplish it within the next week.
- Reward yourself.
- Review your goals. Get excited about them. See yourself achieving them. Take the second action—and you'll be on your way to success!

T

Take Control Of Your Destiny.

We have the power within us to attract all that we could ever want. This power is not based on belief; it is a knowing. This miraculous power goes untapped primarily because of conditioning. We must take control of our own destinies by cultivating this knowing and avoiding clutter and preconceptions that block our paths.

Take control by becoming aware of your higher self. Dreams come true for people who see the invisible. People who see the invisible do what others call impossible. The invisible is the potential inside our bones, arteries, and skin.

We ask ourselves what causes the giant oak tree to become what it is. It progresses from a tiny acorn to a seedling and then a mighty tree. The logical, rational mind suggests that there must be something resembling *treeness* within that acorn. When we open an acorn, we find nothing that resembles a tree. All we find is a mass of brown stuff that looks like dust. Looked at more closely, this dust would reveal molecules, atoms, and subatomic particles. Eventually, we would find waves of energy coming and going mysteriously. That is the invisible potential in all of us.

We become aware of our potential by seeing ourselves as a dimension that transcends the limitations of the physical world— just like that acorn. Once we know we are more than just blood, skin, and bones, we can see our full potential. It starts growing like the mighty oak tree. We attract what we desire. Our ideas come from the highest place—where the invisible becomes visible. That place attracts energy to grow your potential.

Controlling our destinies means taking full responsibility for our lives. Don't blame anyone, including yourself, for any setbacks. We must examine our attitudes about life and rearrange any inner perceptions that don't support who we really are.

You are still growing into your potential. We are more than flesh and bone. We have the same energy inside us as that acorn does. If we control our own destinies, we will reach our goals and experience our full potential. That is success!

Take control of your destiny.

Deliberate Decisions Exercises

- What small successes did you have yesterday that you are thankful for? Write them down.

- Make a renewed commitment today toward your goals. Write it down.

- Write down what kind of legacy you want to leave.

- Create a worksheet to see how you are balancing the roles and activities in your life. Include work, personal, family, friends, community, and your goals. Under personal, list how you are taking care of yourself. Under family, list how you are connecting and spending time with your loved ones. Do the same with your friends. Under work, list how much time you spend at your job. Under community, list your involvement in organizations and activities. Under "your goals," list how much time you are spending on what it takes to achieve them.

- Review your worksheet. Examine how you have scheduled yourself into these different areas of your life. If you think there is an imbalance, write down how you want to reschedule yourself into these different areas. Make the necessary changes to rebalance your life.

U

Understand Yourself To Better Understand Others.

Human beings have the ability to think as well as feel. We must understand and feel feelings—and not just think about feelings. When someone asks how you feel about a certain situation, do you answer with your heart or your head? Too often, we answer with our heads and express our feelings in intellectual ways. We are not really aware of how we feel because we lack self-understanding.

Become aware of your feeling bank. Know yourself more intimately. What makes you happy, sad, glad, melancholy, joyous, or grateful?

Before others can understand us, we must understand ourselves. If we don't, opportunities may pass us by because we will not recognize them. You will be happy when you reach your goal. However, you will be on your journey until you do so. We meet many people on the way who offer us advice to shorten our journeys and bring success closer. Unless we really understand what makes our hearts sing, we may not recognize opportunities. We may miss out on something great.

Trying to *understand* others is another component to "U". Try to understand other people's points of view instead of getting them to see yours. Listen to what they really say—with their words and their hearts. Your relationships will be richer and more harmonious.

Understand yourself to better understand others.

Deliberate Decisions Exercises

- To help you understand yourself a little better, complete the following sentences:

  - "I cry when _____."
  - "I feel sad when _____."

- Think of someone who you know well. Do the same exercise for them. How would they fill in the blanks? See if you can do the second exercise as well. What ten feelings would they choose to fill in those blanks?

- After completing the above exercises, take time to reflect on how you felt doing them and write down your feelings.

  - "I feel frustrated when _____."
  - "I feel resentful when _____."
  - "My heart sings when _____."
  - "I feel impatient when _____."
  - "I feel guilt when _____."
  - "I feel ashamed when _____."
  - "I feel afraid when _____."

- Review your list and add ten more "I feel" statements. Here are some sample keywords:

- Adventurous
- Affectionate
- Agitated
- Alive
- Angry
- Annoyed
- Appreciative
- Blissful
- Bored
- Cheerful
- Complacent
- Confident
- Exhausted
- Fearful
- Helpless
- Hurt
- Inspired
- Irritated
- Jealous
- Joyful
- Lonely
- Mean
- Peaceful
- Proud
- Relieved
- Satisfied
- Stimulated
- Suspicious
- Worried

V

Visualize What You Want.

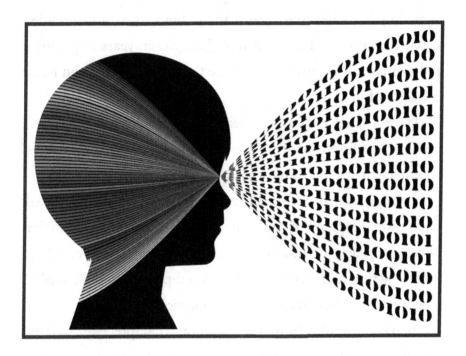

After eleven long years and many obstacles, my daughter Julie graduated from a master's program in speech language pathology. Even though her journey was long with many roadblocks to overcome, she never lost sight of her goal. Julie imagined herself doing what she wanted to do. She created a mental picture of what that looked like and set off on her journey. She started at a community college in her hometown, and then she moved to another city to attend a second community college with the goal of attending a four-year university in that same city.

Julie worked in a bank and then a food mart to pay for her schooling. The university rejected her twice. She continued taking courses at the community college, hoping she would get into the university the following semester. When that did not happen, Julie packed up her bags, moved back to her hometown, and attended another university. Though it took Julie eleven years to graduate and complete her journey, she created a mental picture and never lost sight of it.

Have a fixed goal and a clear picture of your desire. Don't become confused or frustrated by negativity from others. Counteract them by thinking and radiating positive thoughts.

Create a mental picture. Believe with all your heart that it will materialize. People often say, "Believe you can do it and you can. It is done unto you as you believe." Imagination, visualization, creating a mental picture, and believing leads to accomplishment. Belief enables a person to do what others think is impossible.

Behavior results from the thoughts that precede it. If we visualize ourselves as incompetent, we create incompetence. A thought is the first step in the process of visualization. Our entire life experiences revolve around our images of ourselves. Virtually everything we do is a result of the pictures we place in our minds before we attempt anything.

Once we create our mental pictures, we begin converting them into reality. Albert Einstein taught us that time does not exist in the linear world. Time is humankind's invention due to our limited vision and need to compartmentalize everything. There really is no such thing as time. Everything you are capable of visualizing already exists.

We cannot visualize something and then sit around and wait for it to materialize. The opportunity for bringing thought to physical reality is up to us. We must be willing to do whatever it takes to make our mental pictures reality. This is the single most important aspect of visualization. There is no failure. There are only results. Our concept of failure comes from believing someone else's opinion about how we could do something differently

So, dream, dream, and dream more. Visualize your dream. Tell yourself it is already here. Be willing to do whatever is necessary to create a reality from visualization. There is no such thing as failure. There are only results.

We journey toward our dreams by taking steps. It is done unto you as you believe. Success is just one step away!

Visualize what you want.

Deliberate Decisions Exercises

- If you haven't done a "vision board or a dream board", I suggest making one now. Get a poster board, plenty of magazines, a pair of scissors, some glue, markers, crayons, paints, and any other creative aides you might like to use and start creating. Use drawings or pictures from magazines to create a collage of your vision.
- When you have finished your project, put it where you can see it every day. Every time you make a new goal, create another vision board or add it to your existing one.

W

Want It More Than Anything.

Your success depends on the amount of passion you wrap around your goals. Passion is the motivating force that drives us all. When we want something so bad we can taste it, smell it, and feel it, we create it.

The time it takes to reach a goal depends on the degree of passion we feel. Want it more than anything! Many years ago, I invited some Navajo women and their families to join us for the holidays. I didn't realize most of them had never been off their northern Arizona reservation. And it was a nine hundred-mile drive to California. When they told me someone would loan them a camper pickup truck for all eleven of them, I knew they might not make it. I really wanted them to join us for the holidays since they had been so gracious to my family the previous year. I wanted to show the same hospitality to them.

My friends and I put our heads together. All I could think about was getting my friends here with their families. All of sudden, an acquaintance approached me at a function and asked if I was comfortable driving a fifteen-passenger van. I said I was, but I really didn't know if I could. Her husband worked for a car dealership and arranged for a brand-new, never-driven fifteen-passenger van.

I drove the huge van into a blizzard, slid on ice, and almost got stuck in mud on the reservation's dirt roads, but I arrived. My passion and desire to get there got me there more than anything else. I brought back four women and eleven children. With the help of my friends, I arranged gifts for all the children to be under the tree when we arrived back home. My family and I had the best Christmas ever.

Nothing is possible without passion. I wanted it more than anything. It was validation that you can have whatever you want—if you want it more than anything!

Want it more than anything.

Deliberate Decisions Exercises

- Think about the times in your life where passion played a part in achieving what you set out to get or accomplish. Make a list of those times.

- Review your list and put yourself back into those times. Close your eyes and feel what that passion felt like. What did it feel like when you got what you wanted or accomplished what you set out to do? Bring that feeling to the goals and dreams you presently have.

- Hold that passion and renew the excitement about your goals and dreams. Write a paragraph about the passion you currently hold toward your goals and dreams. Read and reread this paragraph until that passion becomes part of you.

X

Xcellerate Your Efforts.

You're almost there. Just a little more to go! Don't slack off as you get closer to achieving your goals. Don't slow down and think you have it made. Keep up the momentum!

Marathon runners start off slowly and increase their speeds as the race goes on. However, as they close in on the finish line, they use their last bit of energy to thrust forward and break that ribbon for the win. As you close in on your finish line, increase your efforts. You will reach your goal. Success is our golden cup and our blue ribbon.

We use the tools we acquire along the way to help us "xcellerate" our efforts. Spend more time on whatever needs doing. Give up an hour of television or get up an hour earlier. Do whatever it takes to propel yourself to the finish line. Go back and read these ABCs. Use E for *excitement*. Get excited about almost being there. Remember J—and just take action!

We're close to the last letter of our ABCs. Success is just around the corner.

Xcellerate your efforts.

Deliberate Decisions Exercises

- Today or tomorrow, determine where could you find an extra hour to work on your goals. Write down where you could find an extra hour every day this week. Maybe watch television an hour less or get up an hour earlier.
- Take these extra hours and use them to work toward your goals. Write down some action steps you could take—and then take them.

W

Yesterday Is Gone. Tomorrow May Not Come. Today Is All You Have.

Don't live in the past! Don't cry over spilled milk. The past is over. The check is cashed. Let go of whatever has happened in the past. It holds us back from continuing on the journey to success. You are the author of your life. Write a new chapter. You cannot rewrite the past.

Avoid living in the future too! The future may not look the way you think it will. People often say, "The check is in the mail." You don't have that check in your hand—and you may never get it.

Today is all you have. The present. Now. You received the check, cashed it, and have the money in your hand. Avoid wasting today by reliving the past or daydreaming about future success. Make a call, write that overdue letter, or think big by writing a business plan or finishing an overdue project.

Success depends on what we do today. The actions we take today help us write the next chapter of our lives. We cannot relive the past. Yesterday is gone. Tomorrow may not come. Daydreaming about the future without action is a waste of precious time. We could spend that time doing something to make our dreams a reality.

You are the author of your life. Start writing your next chapter today. Live in the present.

Yesterday is gone. Tomorrow may not come. Today is all you have.

Deliberate Decisions Exercises

- If you find yourself trying to relive the past or daydreaming about the future, do something different than your normal routine right away. This will help you change your thought patterns. Changing your thought patterns will interrupt your obsession with the past and keep you from daydreaming about the future.
- What are some things you could do differently today? Write them down. For the next week, practice them.

Z

Zero In On Your Target—
And Go For It!

This is the last letter in our *Deliberate Decisions ABC* series.

There are times we have a target, a goal, or a dream that does not come to pass. Why didn't I reach it? Why did I stop short just as I was getting close? Was I afraid? Did I lack commitment? If the answer was "yes" to any of those questions, take a good look at what stopped you.

Zeroing in on a target requires commitment, certainty, and willingness.

Commitment is an intention and not just an idea. Stopping short translates into a lack of commitment. Is this really what you want in life? Are you really committed to your goal? Are you willing to do what it takes to stay committed to it?

Commitment means change. Are you ready for change? Are you afraid to make the changes that will come from reaching your target? There is a big difference between interest and commitment. "I would like to make more money." "I would like to own my own home." "I would really like to make a difference in the world." These statements are not commitments at all. They are statements of a preference. They say, "I'm interested in having this happen if I don't have to do anything." It does not come from the powerful place inside us. It comes from a weak plea made without the energy to launch it.

In 1955, a young black woman stepped onto a bus in Montgomery, Alabama. She refused to give up her seat to a white person as she was legally required. That moment was the beginning of the civil rights movement. Was Rosa Parks thinking of the future when she refused to relinquish her seat on that bus? Did she have a divine plan for how she could change the structure of society? Perhaps. Her commitment to hold herself to a higher standard compelled her to act. What a far-reaching effect one woman's commitment has made by not giving up her seat.

If we have clear convictions and strong spiritual or religious paths, we can hold tight to our goals and zero in on our targets. We can rid ourselves of the fears that block us from doing so. By staying on our chosen spiritual paths and trusting in a power greater than ourselves, we will get out of our own ways. Commit to a goal, state it as an intention, zero in on the target, and allow the power inside to take over.

Make a deliberate decision to commit to your dream. Walk your chosen path with conviction. If you commit to your goal, you will hit the bull's-eye. Zero in and go for it!

Zero in on your target—and go for it!

Deliberate Decisions Exercises

- Draw a target and put your goal or dream in the bull's-eye. Draw arrows in the different rings to indicate your progress.
- Each time you take an action toward your goal, move or add an arrow to the next ring closer to the bull's-eye.
- Write your commitment and intention on a piece of paper and place it next to your goal in the bull's-eye.
- When your arrow hits the bull's-eye, celebrate!

Bibliography

Bristol, Claude M. (1985), *The Magic of Believing: The Science of Setting Your Goal and Then Reaching It.* Prentice Hall, New York, NY

Brussat, Frederic and Mary Ann (1996) *Spiritual Literacy: Reading the Sacred in Everyday Life.* Simon and Schuster, New York, NY

Brussat, Frederic and Mary Ann (2000) *Spiritual Rx: Prescriptions for Living a Meaningful Life.* Hyperion, NY Butterworth, Eric (1983)

Butterworth, Eric. *Spiritual Economics: The Prosperity Process.* Unity School of Christianity, Unity Village, MO

Canfield, Jack and Mark Victor Hanson (1994) *Dare to Win.* Berkley, New York, NY

Chopra, Deepak (1994) *The Seven Spiritual Laws of Success: A Practical Guide to the Fulfillment of your Dreams.* Copublished by Amber-Allen and New World Library, San Rafael, CA

Covey, Stephen R. (1989) *The 7 Habits of Highly Effective People: Powerful Lessons in Personal Change.* Simon & Schuster, Inc., New York, NY

Cole-Whitaker, Terry (1979) *What You Think of Me is None of My Business.* A. S. Barnes and Co., Inc., San Diego, CA

Dyer, Dr. Wayne (1992) *Real Magic: Creating Miracles in Everyday Life*. Harper Collins Publishers, Inc., New York, NY

Dyer, Dr. Wayne (1997) M*anifest Your Destiny: The Nine Spiritual Principles for Getting Everything You Want*. Harper Collins Publishers, Inc., New York, NY

Dyer, Dr. Wayne (2004) *The Power of Intention, Learning to Co-create Your World Your Way*. Hay House, Inc. Carlsbad, CA

Hanh, Thich Nhat (1975) *The Miracle of Mindfulness: A Manual on Meditation*. Beacon Press, Boston, MA

Patent, Arnold M. (1991) *You Can Have it All*. Celebration Publishing, Sylva, NC

Robbins, Anthony (1993) *Awaken the Giant Within: How to Take Immediate Control of Your Mental, Emotional, Physical and Financial Destiny*. Simon & Schuster, New York, NY

Roger, John and Peter McWilliams (1988) *You Can't Afford the Luxury of a Negative Thought*. Prelude Press, Los Angeles, CA

Tolle, Eckhart (1999) *The Power of Now: A Guide to Spiritual Enlightenment*. New World Library, Novato, CA

Printed in the United States
By Bookmasters